KU-575-714

Tiger Talk
My Day Out

At the Swimming Pool

Leon Read

W
FRANKLIN WATTS
LONDON•SYDNEY

Contents

Look out for Tiger on the pages of this book. Sometimes he is hiding.

Today, Beth is going to the swimming pool with her mum and dad.

Getting ready

Beth packs her bag.

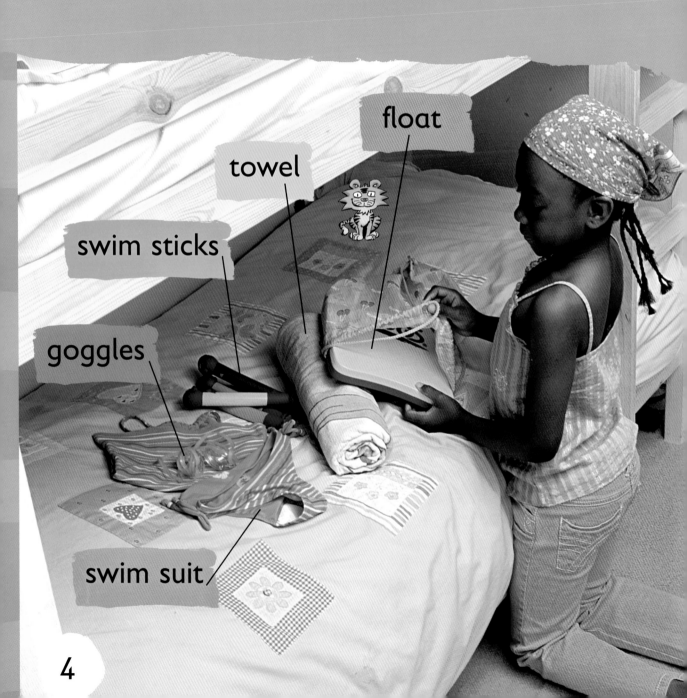

float

towel

swim sticks

goggles

swim suit

Mum puts the bags in the car.

Dad is going to drive to the pool.

Put on your seatbelt please.

At the pool

Mum buys three tickets.

Then they
go into the
changing room.

Beth, Mum and
Dad put on their
swimming clothes.

Beth chooses a locker.
She puts the bags inside.

Why does Dad need
to keep the locker
key safe?

Pool safety

There are rules at the pool to keep people safe.

Beth walks along the edge.

A lifeguard watches people in the pool.

ATTENTION!

SWIM SAFELY

RULES:

- Do not run
- Do not behave in a dangerous way
- Young swimmers must be supervised by an adult
- Shower after your swim

ENJOY YOUR SWIM

What other places have safety rules?

Come on in!

The air inside the swimming pool is very warm but the water feels chilly!

The water feels warm when you swim.

How does the water feel when you get in the pool?

Shallow and deep

Beth and Mum stay at the shallow end.

Beth does not like the deep end.

No Diving

Why is this sign at the shallow end?

Dad is at the deep end.

Tiger and Rabbit are watching him.

DEEP END

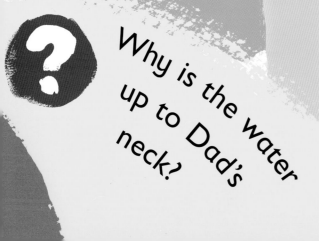

? Why is the water up to Dad's neck?

13

Splashing about

Beth loves splashing with her legs.

I kick the water to make it foamy.

Beth
splashes
Dad.

Mum
splashes
Dad.

Why should you stop splashing when someone asks you to?

Float fun

Beth uses a float to practise kicking.

She holds the float between
her legs to practise paddling.

What ways do
you use a float?

17

Swimming lessons

Beth has swimming lessons.

Before Beth could swim, she wore armbands like her friend Lotty.

Now Beth can swim using her arms and legs.

Beth has her first swim certificate and badge.

Do you have swimming lessons?

Water game

Beth is playing a game with swim sticks.

Her swim sticks sink to the
bottom of the pool.

Beth has to go underwater to get them. She holds her breath.

Why does Beth hold her breath underwater?

21

Swimming sports

There are lots of swimming sports you can do.

Some people race each other.

Some people play games.

This game is called water polo.

What other things can you do in water?

Word picture bank

Armbands – P. 18

Float – P. 16

Lifeguard – P. 9

Locker key – P. 7

Swim badge – P. 19

Water polo – P. 23

First published in 2008 by Franklin Watts
338 Euston Road, London NW1 3BH

Franklin Watts Australia
Level 17/207 Kent Street, Sydney NSW 2000

Copyright © Franklin Watts 2008

Series editor: Adrian Cole
Photographer: Andy Crawford (unless otherwise credited)
Design: Sphere Design Associates
Art director: Jonathan Hair
Consultants: Prue Goodwin and Karina Law

A CIP catalogue record for this book is available
from the British Library.

ISBN: 978 0 7496 7621 6

Dewey Classification: 797.2'1

Acknowledgements:
The Publisher would like to thank Norrie Carr model agency
and the staff at Mile End Leisure Centre and Stadium.
'Tiger' and 'Rabbit' puppets used with kind permission from
Ravensden PLC (www.ravensden.co.uk).
Tiger Talk logo drawn by Kevin Hopgood.

Shutterstock (18, 22, 23, 24tl and br).

Every attempt has been made to clear copyright.
Should there be any inadvertent omission please
apply to the publisher for rectification.

Printed in China

Franklin Watts is a division
of Hachette Children's Books,
an Hachette Livre UK company.

There are 17 Tigers, including me, in this book.
Did you find all of us?